TRIBES of NATIVE AMERICA

Zuñi Pueblo

edited by Marla Felkins Ryan
and Linda Schmittroth

BLACKBIRCH®
PRESS

San Diego • Detroit • New York • San Francisco • Cleveland
New Haven, Conn. • Waterville, Maine • London • Munich

THOMSON
＊
GALE

For more information, contact
The Gale Group, Inc.
27500 Drake Rd.
Farmington Hills, MI 48331-3535
Or you can visit our Internet site at http://www.gale.com

Photo credits: Cover © Blackbirch Press Archives; cover Courtesy of Northwestern University Library; cover © National Archives; cover © Perry Jasper Photography; cover © Photospin; cover © PhotoDisc; cover © Picturequest; cover © Seattle Post-Intelligencer Collection, Museum of History & Industry; pages 5, 9, 13, 24 © Denver Public Library, Western History Department; pages 6, 10, 11, 12, 13, 14, 15, 16, 17, 18 (both images), 23, 25, 26, 28 © CORBIS; pages 7, 22 © Corel Corporation; pages 8, 15, 19 (both images), 20, 21 (both images), © nativestock.com; page 9 © Art Resource; page 27 © North Wind Picture Archives

LIBRARY OF CONGRESS CATALOGING-IN-PUBLICATION DATA

Zuñi Pueblo / Marla Felkins Ryan, book editor; Linda Schmittroth, book editor.
 v. cm. — (Tribes of Native America)
Includes bibliographical references and index.
Contents: Name — History — Religion — Government — Daily life — Arts.
 ISBN 1-56711-617-5 (hardback : alk. paper)
 1. Zuñi Pueblo Indians—Juvenile literature. [1. Zuñi Pueblo Indians. 2. Indians of North America—Southwest.] I. Ryan, Marla Felkins. II. Schmittroth, Linda. III. Series.
 E99.P9 P83 203
 978.9004'974—dc21   2002007856

Printed in United States
10 9 8 7 6 5 4 3 2 1

Table of Contents

ZUÑI PUEBLO

Name

Zuñi (*ZOON-yee*) Pueblo. The Zuñi call themselves
A'shiwi, or "the flesh." They call their pueblo—the town
where they live—*Itiwana,* which means "middle place."

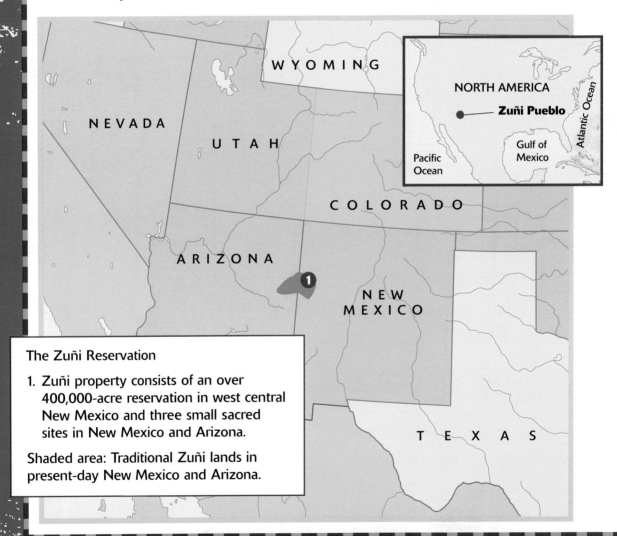

WYOMING

NEVADA

UTAH

NORTH AMERICA

Zuñi Pueblo

Pacific
Ocean

Gulf of
Mexico

Atlantic Ocean

COLORADO

ARIZONA

①

NEW
MEXICO

TEXAS

The Zuñi Reservation

1. Zuñi property consists of an over
400,000-acre reservation in west central
New Mexico and three small sacred
sites in New Mexico and Arizona.

Shaded area: Traditional Zuñi lands in
present-day New Mexico and Arizona.

Where are the traditional Zuñi lands?

The over 400,000-acre Zuñi federal reservation is in west central New Mexico. The Zuñi also have three smaller pieces of sacred land in New Mexico and Arizona.

Zuñi Pueblo, New Mexico. The Zuñi have sacred lands in New Mexico and Arizona.

What has happened to the population?

In 1540, there were about 6,000 Zuñi. In the late 1700s, there were 1,600 to 1,900. In 1850, there were about 1,300. In a 1990 population count by the U.S. Bureau of the Census, 8,281 people said that they were Zuñi.

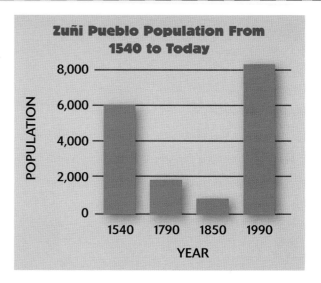

Zuñi Pueblo Population From 1540 to Today

Zuñi girls at a powwow. From 1850 to 1990, the number of people who called themselves Zuñi grew by nearly 7,000.

Origins and group ties

Zuñi tales say that their ancestors had webbed feet, long ears, hairless tails, and moss-covered bodies. They took on human form after they bathed in a sacred spring.

The Zuñi are one of the largest of the Pueblo tribes, both in terms of people and land.

The Zuñi have lived in the Southwest for more than 2,000 years.

HISTORY

The Spanish arrive

For more than 2,000 years, the Zuñi people have lived in the Zuñi and Little Colorado River valleys of the Southwest. By around A.D. 1250, people from California to the Great Plains and into Mexico traded on Zuñi land. Items such as corn, salt, turquoise, cotton cloth, and jewelry were traded for macaw feathers, seashells, coral, and copper.

The Zuñi traded items for feathers from the macaw.

The Zuñi first met whites in the mid-1500s. Spaniards entered Zuñi villages as they searched for gold and riches. These early meetings were not friendly. Fights broke out, and people on both sides were killed.

Retreat from invaders

The Spaniards stayed at the Zuñi villages, even after the fights. The unhappy Zuñi encouraged the Spaniards to explore other regions. When they could no longer avoid conflicts with the Spanish, the Zuñi moved to Thunder Mountain. This 1,000-foot-high hill had steep sides and a flat top.

During the 16th and 17th centuries, the Navajo, Apache, and other tribes destroyed all the Zuñi villages. Then, the Spanish returned in 1692 and reclaimed the area for Mexico. They convinced the Zuñi to accept Spanish rule. The people came down from Thunder Mountain and began to build a new Zuñi pueblo.

The Zuñi fight Spanish explorers who arrived in the mid-1500s. Battles between the Zuñi and whites killed many people on both sides.

1861
American Civil War begins

1865
Civil War ends

1869
The Transcontinental Railroad is completed

1877
A Zuñi reservation is set up

1941
Bombing at Pearl Harbor forces United States into WWII

1978
The U.S. government gives the sacred Zuñi Salt Lake back to the tribe

1984
The U.S. government gives the sacred area called Zuñi Heaven in eastern Arizona back to the tribe

1917–1918
WWI fought in Europe

1929
Stock market crash begins the Great Depression

The Spanish leave

Many Zuñi made silver jewelry to support themselves after they lost much of their land.

In 1703, the Zuñi killed three Spanish officials because of their rude behavior. For more than 100 years after that, the Spanish usually left the Zuñi alone.

In 1820, the Spanish left Zuñi Pueblo for good. The tribe had refused to adopt European ways, even after nearly 300 years of Spanish influence.

Taken over

After Mexico rebelled against Spain in the early 19th century, it could not afford to send soldiers to watch over its northern frontier. This area included Zuñi land. The Zuñi began to trade with the United States. Within 25 years, the United States took over the region. In 1877, the United States set up a reservation for the Zuñi.

In the 1870s, a railroad was built in the region. This made it possible to ship animals. The Zuñi began to raise and sell sheep and cattle. By the late 1890s, many whites, including teachers, missionaries, traders, and government officials, lived with the Zuñi.

A century of hardships

Whites brought new diseases, and many Zuñi died in smallpox epidemics. By the end of the 19th century, the Zuñi had lost much

Many Zuñi made silver jewelry to support themselves after they lost much of their land.

of their land to settlers and railroad builders. They could no longer raise crops and livestock. To survive, many Zuñi began to make silver jewelry.

Life improves

By the 20th century, the Zuñi suffered severe health problems and were worried about land claims. They were also concerned about education for their children. Conditions had begun to improve for the Zuñi by the end of the century. As better health care became available, the population finally grew to be higher than it was when the Zuñi first met the Spanish. Since 1978, the tribe has won back its sacred Zuñi Salt Lake. The tribe also regained control of an area called Zuñi Heaven. The spirits of the Zuñi people are believed to live in this area after death. In 1980, the reservation set up its own public school district.

Our Lady of Guadalupe Mission. Today, many Zuñi are Christian, though traditional Zuñi religion is still important.

Religion

The Zuñi had many gods, but their supreme being was the sun. The Zuñi also admired the keen senses, sharp teeth, claws, talons, cleverness, and quickness of animals. They believed animals were closer to the spirit world than people were.

Today, many Zuñi are part of Christian churches, but the traditional Zuñi religion is still very important. Some parts of the traditional religion are kept secret.

Government

For centuries, the Zuñi pueblo was run by men called bow priests. They were in charge of a priestly council. During the 1890s, the United States put bow priests in jail to end the tribe's ancient religious and political system. By 1934, the Zuñi could no longer choose their governor and tribal council in their own way. Over the decades that followed, the religious Zuñi government became a non-religious democratic government. By 1970, the tribe had written a constitution. Today, the Zuñi Tribal Council governs the reservation.

Officials in Zuñi Pueblo, New Mexico. Until the 1890s, the Zuñi ran their own government.

The loss of agriculture

The Zuñi people were once farmers. After the move to the reservation, the Zuñi had less land. This made it hard to grow enough crops to survive.

Between 1911 and 1988, the number of acres farmed at the Zuñi pueblo fell by 83 percent. By the late 1990s, only about 1,000 acres were farmed, while 95 percent of the tribal land was used to graze livestock.

The Zuñi grew crops in Zuñi Pueblo (pictured). In the late 1990s, only 5 percent of tribal land was used for farming.

Jobs in modern times

Today, sheep are a major source of income on the reservation. The tribe's herd numbers around 14,000. The Zuñi also tend peach orchards. They have about 2,000 cattle, as well as hogs, pigs, fowl, horses, and goats.

Sheep are a major source of income on the Zuñi reservation.

Zuñi jeweler
Chester Mahooty
displays some of
his work.

The tribal government is the reservation's main employer. Most Zuñi small businesses involve arts and crafts. Crafters make jewelry, pottery, paintings, and beadwork. By the 1960s, 90 percent of the tribe's members were silver crafters at least part of the time.

Small businesses on the Zuñi reservation sell pottery as well as other arts and crafts.

The Zuñi were the first group of Native Americans trained as firefighting experts. The U.S. Forest Service often sends Zuñi to put out the nation's worst forest fires.

Since the 1960s, the tribe has received nearly $50 million in court cases over land claims. They have used this money to improve tribal income and education.

The Zuñi were the first group of Native Americans to be trained as firefighting experts.

DAILY LIFE

The roles of men and women

In Zuñi tradition, men were the farmers, herdsmen, and hunters. They kept the gods happy, while the women took care of the family and tribe. Women prepared food offerings for the gods, and presented special foods to ancestors at each meal. Women greeted the sunrise and made bodies ready for burial. Men carved and painted sticks adorned with feathers and shells, to be offered to the gods. They also organized ceremonies and played the roles of spirits in ritual dances.

A Zuñi woman grinds corn. Women prepared food offerings for Zuñi gods.

By the late 1800s, most Zuñi lived in dwellings like this one in New Mexico.

Buildings

As late as the end of the 19th century, most Zuñi lived in traditional "apartment houses" that stood five stories high. Today, many Zuñi live in single-family homes. Houses may be modern in style. But they are often built with the same kind of stone the Zuñi have used for centuries.

Clothing

Zuñi men usually wore breechcloths (flaps of material that covered the front and back). These had fringed edges and a tassel at each corner that was tied over the hips. Men sometimes added long robes of feathers and the skins of hares, or cotton blankets. The women wore mantas (MAHN-tuhs).

Zuñi men wore breechcloths, and women wore dresses called mantas.

To make these dresses, women used a rectangular piece of dark blue or black cotton or wool. The material was wrapped around the body, passed under the left arm, and tied above the right shoulder. A sash encircled the waist. Women also wore boot-like moccasins topped with leggings made of strips of deerskin.

Food

For hundreds of years, the Zuñi watered their farms using small dams and canals. These sent rainwater to the crops but kept them safe from floods. The Zuñi even came up with a way to protect their crops from birds. They strung cactus leaves on lines that crisscrossed the fields. The leaves waved in the

Corn was the major crop of the Zuñi.

wind and frightened birds. At times, children and elderly people also made noise and threw stones at invading birds.

Corn was the major crop. The Zuñi may have grown up to 10,000 acres of it at a time. In a good year, they grew enough to feed the people for two

The Zuñi gathered and ate wild nuts and fruits.

years, in case of a drought or other disaster. The Zuñi raised corn, beans, and garden vegetables. They hunted wild game such as rabbits, deer, and bears. They also fished, and gathered wild nuts and fruits.

Education

Today, the Zuñi have their own school system. The schools teach language and cultural history, and support tribal customs in many ways. For example, some students must eat a special diet because they are involved in tribal initiation rites. These students are given special lunches. Classes are also canceled if there is an important festival.

Healing practices

The Zuñi are known for their beadwork on dolls, belts, and necklaces.

Both men and women may join Zuñi medicine societies. Some societies use spiritual methods to cure. Others use medical techniques. Members learn how plants, roots, massage, and healing rituals work.

In earlier times, some Zuñi medicine societies staged displays to bring good health to the community. In these shows, performers swallowed fire or swords, or danced over hot coals. Many ailments were thought to be caused by spirits and witches. Zuñi healers thought to cure such a problem, they might have to remove something put inside the body by a supernatural being. This item could be a pebble, feather, or wood particle.

Zuñi artisans carve animal figures from stone.

Arts

The Zuñi make beautiful jewelry out of turquoise, shell, and jet that is set in silver. Tribal members are also known for their fine beadwork on belts, necklaces, and figures. They also carve animals from shells and stone. The most popular Zuñi pottery is white with a reddish-brown design.

A Zuñi canteen. White pottery with a reddish-brown design is a popular Zuñi style.

THE CORN RACE

Long ago, when people first came to live in this world, everybody did the same kind of work. When the twin brothers wanted to give the Indians the gift of corn they talked it over. Morning Star said, "It would be better to give the corn to one group— not to all." So they tried to think of a plan. Morning Star said, "I know what we can do. We can have a corn race and see which will be the corn raisers. Let us call all the people."

When all the people had gathered he chose the fastest runner from each tribe—one Zuñi, one Acoma, and one Navaho. He took an ear of corn out of his belt and broke it into three parts, the butt being the largest part, the middle piece a little smaller, and the point the smallest of all. He placed them on the ground with the point nearest the runners, the middle part next and the largest piece at the back.

At last all was ready. The signal was given and they were off. They ran as lightly as the deer and as swiftly. The people watched breathlessly. The racers drew apart with the Navaho boy in the lead. As he rushed past the goal he snatched up the first piece of corn which was the point. The Acoma racer came in next and he took the middle piece. The Zuñi boy, coming in

Zuñi legends say Evening Star designated the Zuñi and the Acoma as the tribes to raise corn.

last, got the butt end of the ear.

The elder brother shook his head and said, "The Navaho won the race. He should have got the largest piece of corn. Instead he has the smallest." But Evening Star replied, "It is well. The Navaho is the swiftest runner. He will always be moving about from place to place. He will not be able to take care of much corn. The people of Zuñi and Acoma will live in houses. They will stay in one place so they can raise much corn."

And so it has been just as the Evening Star said. The Navaho are always moving. They have their summer homes and their winter homes. But the Zuñi and Acoma are still living in their pueblos and make their living mostly by farming.

According to legend, the Navajo are swifter runners than the Acoma or Zuñi.

SOURCE: Edgar L. Hewett. "The Corn Race." *Ancient Life in the American Southwest.* 1930. Reprint, Indianapolis: Biblo and Tannen, 1968.

CUSTOMS

Clans

Every Zuñi is part of a clan, a group that traces its ancestry to the same person. Clan membership comes from the mother, but families also have ties to the father's clan. Zuñi clans are in a constant state of change. As some die out, others grow larger.

Festivals

Zuñi Shalako ceremony. During this ceremony, Zuñi celebrate the new year and also bless new houses.

The most dramatic annual event at the Zuñi pueblo is the Shalako ceremony. It celebrates the new year

and blesses new houses. It is not open to the public, but several other annual events are. Among these are the June Rain Dance, held in August, and the Zuñi Tribal Fair, a celebration held over Labor Day weekend.

Courtship and marriage

Zuñi courtship was complicated. When a young man wanted to marry a young woman, he let her know that he liked her. He asked her if she had the same feelings for him. If she did, she asked her mother whether the man was a suitable mate. If her family approved, the young couple met several times in secret to decide if they did want to wed. During this time, either person could call off the engagement. If the woman called it off, nothing else happened. If the man called it off, however, he had to pay a "bride price" to her family.

A Zuñi dancer wears special clothing for the White Buffalo Dance. Dance is an important part of many Zuñi rituals.

If the woman refused the bride price, she could "go public" with her intentions to marry him.

To go public meant that the young woman went to the young man's home. She gave his mother a gift. If the mother liked the young woman, she presented

A Zuñi couple in Albuquerque, New Mexico. A man or woman was able to call off a wedding engagement at any time during their courtship.

THE SHALAKO CEREMONY (HOUSE BLESSING CEREMONY)

The most spectacular annual Zuñi ceremony involves the Shalakos. They are men dressed as ten-to-twelve-foot-tall messenger birds. These men act out the annual visit of the birds to bring blessings to the Zuñi people.

Each year on a late December afternoon, the Zuñi hear the cries of the approaching Shalakos. The birds begin to cross the small river that runs through the pueblo. Then the crowds of people who have gathered together in the Zuñi village square fall silent.

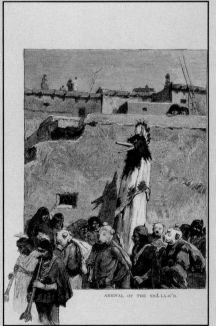

ARRIVAL OF THE SHÁ-LA-K'O.

Men dress as tall messenger birds during the Zuñi Shalako ceremony.

Rhythmic jingles in the distance grow louder, and finally the majestic Shalakos stride into the square.

These commanding, colorful creatures have wide eyes, buffalo horns, and ruffs of raven feathers beneath their dome-shaped, beaked heads. They wear brilliant masks of bright red, turquoise, and black. They also wear beautiful jewelry, rattles, ankle bells, and pine boughs. Through their prayers, the Shalakos honor all living and nonliving things in the universe. As the creatures circle the village square, masked singers chant. The air rings with the rhythmic sounds of drums, bells, rattles, and the clacking of wooden bird beaks as they open and close. Then the Shalakos bend their knees and begin their classic back-and-forth dancing. They dance to awaken the earth and stir the clouds. They do this in hopes that they will bring on the rain that is so necessary to the parched land of the Zuñi.

Zuñi people of all ages attend rituals such as the Shalako ceremony.

Visitors were once welcome to watch the Shalako ceremony, but were asked not to record their observations. In recent times, the crowds of visitors became so large that they did not allow the Zuñi to enter the new houses in the pueblo and carry out their blessing ritual. As a result, this event has been closed to non-Indians since 1995.

her with wedding finery: a traditional black dress, moccasins, shawl, and beads. If the man then had a change of heart, he went to the girl's home with her. If he still did not want to marry her, she could move into his home and stay until he changed his mind or until she became ashamed. At that point, she gave the wedding finery back to his mother and returned to her family home.

If neither person called off the engagement, the woman ground corn as a gift for her mother-in-law. Then, the man brought his wife to his mother, who gave her the wedding finery. The couple went back to the bride's home, and the man spent the night. He then left in daylight so that the new marriage would be known to all.

Death

A body was buried the day after death, but the spirit was thought to stay in the home for four days. When a person died, he or she was no longer mentioned by name. Silent prayers could be said in his or her memory, though.

Current tribal issues

Buildings that make up the old Zuñi Middle Village at the center of the pueblo rest on ruins below. Because the old structures are now crumbling, walls and floors in the occupied rooms above them crack and slope.

Ceremonial dances take place in this area. Hundreds of people gather to watch. This puts even more pressure on the decaying foundation. As a result, a number of homes and ceremonial areas are in danger of collapsing. To make the foundations stronger will take a lot of work. In the late 1990s, the Zuñi Tribal Council planned to ask the U.S. Congress for $2.5 million to make the repairs.

The return of religious sites

The Zuñi have won back two of their main religious sites, Zuñi Salt Lake and Zuñi Heaven. They have also received cash from the government for tribal lands that were illegally sold or were damaged. This money has helped the tribe begin a project to fix damaged lands.

Notable people

Edmund Ladd (1926–) was the first Zuñi to earn a college degree. In the paper he wrote to get his Ph.D., he talked about the roles of birds and feathers in Zuñi mythology and religion. He has worked as an archaeologist for the National Park Service. He was also an official at the Museum of New Mexico in Santa Fe.

Other notable Zuñi include painter Kai Sa (1918–1974), also known as Percy Sandy; jewelry designer Rod Kaskalla (1955–), and Roger Tsabetsye (1941–), an artist.

For More Information

Bonvillain, Nancy. *The Zuñi.* New York: Chelsea House Publishers, 1995.

Button, Bertha P. *Friendly People: The Zuñi Indians.* Santa Fe, NM: Museum of New Mexico Press, 1963.

Ferguson, T. J., and Cal A. Seciwa. "Zuñi." *Native America in the Twentieth Century: An Encyclopedia.* Ed. Mary B. Davis. New York: Garland Publishing, 1994.

Hirschfelder, Arlene, and Martha Kreipe de Montaño. *The Native American Almanac: A Portrait of Native America Today.* New York: Prentice Hall, 1993.

People of the Desert. Alexandria, VA: Time-Life Books, 1993.

Sando, Joe S. *Pueblo Nations: Eight Centuries of Pueblo Indian History.* Santa Fe, NM: Clear Light Publishers, 1992.

Terrell, John Upton. *Pueblos, Gods, & Spaniards.* New York: Dial Press, 1973.

Through Indian Eyes: The Untold Story of Native American Peoples. Pleasantville, NY: Readers Digest Association, 1995.

Trimble, Stephen. *The People: Indians of the American Southwest.* Santa Fe, NM: School of American Research Press, 1993.

Glossary

Adorn decorate with

Reservation land set aside and given to Native Americans

Ritual something that is custom or done in a certain way

Sacred highly valued and important

Tradition a custom or an established pattern of behavior

Treaty agreement

Tribe a group of people who live together in a community

Index